SCHOLASTIC

Success With

Grammar

D1406765

New York • Toronto • London • Auckland • Sydney
Mexico City • New Delhi • Hong Kong • Buenos Aires

Teaching
Resources

State Standards Correlations

To find out how this book helps you meet your state's standards, log on to **www.scholastic.com/ssw**

Cover design by Ka-Yeon Kim-Li

ISBN 978-0-545-20104-9

20   40   20 19 18 17

TABLE OF CONTENTS

INTRODUCTION

"Nothing Succeeds Like Success."
—Alexandre Dumas the Elder, 1854

And no other resource boosts kids' grammar skills like *Scholastic Success With Grammar*! For classroom or at-home use, this exciting series for kids in grades 1 through 5 provides invaluable reinforcement and practice in grammar topics such as:

- sentence types
- parts of speech
- common and proper nouns
- sentence structure
- verb tenses
- subject-verb agreement
- punctuation
- capitalization
  and more!

This 64-page book contains loads of practice pages to keep kids challenged and excited as they strengthen the grammar skills they need to read and write well.

For each topic, you'll also find an assessment sheet that gives kids realistic practice in taking standardized tests—and helps you see their progress!

What makes *Scholastic Success With Grammar* so solid?
Each practice page in the series reinforces a specific, age-appropriate skill as outlined in one or more standardized tests. Take the lead and help kids succeed with *Scholastic Success With Grammar*. Parents and teachers agree: No one helps kids succeed like Scholastic.

TYPES OF SENTENCES

RETEACHING: A **declarative sentence** makes a statement. An **interrogative sentence** asks a question. An **exclamatory sentence** shows strong feeling. An **imperative sentence** states a command.

A. What kind of sentence is each of the following? Write *declarative, interrogative, exclamatory,* or *imperative* on the line.

1. Merlin carried the baby to safety. _____

2. Why did traitors poison the town's wells? _____

3. Go back and fetch the missing sword. _____

4. Slip the sword into the groove, and pull it out. _____

5. The king was England's bravest ruler! _____

6. Who will follow Selene? _____

B. Identify which groups of words are incomplete sentences and which are complete sentences. Write *incomplete* or *complete* on the line.

1. Sarah at the edge of the square. _____

2. The knights fought so bravely! _____

3. How did Kay treat her dog? _____

4. The sword out of the stone. _____

5. Natalie was trained to be a pilot. _____

C. Correct the incomplete sentences in part B. Add an action word to each one. Then rewrite the complete sentence on the line.

1. _____

2. _____

TYPES OF SENTENCES

A. Add the correct end punctuation mark to each sentence. Then write *declarative, interrogative, exclamatory,* or *imperative* to tell what kind of sentence it is.

1. How do turtles protect themselves_ _____

2. What heavy, hot suits of steel they wore_ _____

3. Pretend that you are an acrobat or juggler_ _____

4. The students sang songs, told stories, and recited poems_ _____

B. Use one of the words below to complete each sentence. Then identify each sentence by writing *declarative, interrogative, exclamatory,* or *imperative.*

> pass   won   listened   play

1. The audience _____ to the bagpipes. _____

2. What kind of games did pioneers like
   to _____? _____

3. Please _____ me the pepper. _____

4. I've _____ three chess games in a row! _____

C. Write an example of a declarative, interrogative, exclamatory, and imperative sentence. Be sure to use the correct end punctuation.

1. Declarative: _____

2. Interrogative: _____

3. Exclamatory: _____

4. Imperative: _____

TYPES OF SENTENCES

Decide if there is an error in the underlined part of each sentence.
Fill in the bubble next to the correct answer.

1. <u>you do like</u> to see movies about knights and castles?

    ⓐ You do like
    ⓑ Do you like
    ⓒ correct as is

2. Please hand me that mystery book about <u>the Middle Ages?</u>

    ⓐ the Middle Ages!
    ⓑ the Middle Ages.
    ⓒ correct as is

3. Grandfather described life in the early part <u>of the century.</u>

    ⓐ of the century?
    ⓑ of the century!
    ⓒ correct as is

4. Why don't you write about <u>your life!</u>

    ⓐ your life?
    ⓑ your life.
    ⓒ correct as is

5. <u>Begin by describing</u> your very first memory.

    ⓐ begin by describing
    ⓑ By describing
    ⓒ correct as is

6. I had such fun swimming <u>in the ocean?</u>

    ⓐ in the ocean
    ⓑ in the ocean!
    ⓒ correct as is

7. What do you remember about your first day <u>in school?</u>

    ⓐ in school!
    ⓑ in school.
    ⓒ correct as is

8. <u>another story</u> about our relatives in Mexico.

    ⓐ Tell me another story
    ⓑ Another story
    ⓒ correct as is

9. The fish looked so colorful swimming in <u>the Caribbean Sea</u>

    ⓐ the Caribbean Sea!
    ⓑ the Caribbean Sea?
    ⓒ correct as is

10. He told us about <u>his trip?</u>

    ⓐ his trip
    ⓑ his trip.
    ⓒ correct as is

SIMPLE AND COMPLETE SUBJECTS AND PREDICATES

> **RETEACHING:** The **simple subject** is the main noun or pronoun that tells whom or what the sentence is about. The **complete subject** is the simple subject and all of the words that go with it. The **simple predicate** is the verb that tells what the subject does or is. The **complete predicate** is the verb and all the words that tell what the subject does or is.

A. Draw a line between the complete subject and the complete predicate. Underline the complete subject once and the simple subject twice.

1. A small family lived on a faraway planet.

2. The family's two children played near the space launch.

3. The little girl dreamed about life on Earth.

4. Huge spaceships landed daily on the planet.

5. The spaceship mechanics repaired huge cargo ships.

6. Twinkling stars appeared in the black sky.

B. Draw a line between the complete subject and the complete predicate. Underline the complete predicate once and the simple predicate twice.

1. The planet's inhabitants lived in underground homes.

2. A special machine manufactures air inside the family's home.

3. The athletic girl jumped high into the air.

4. Many toys and games cluttered the children's playroom.

5. The children's father described weather on Earth.

C. Circle the complete subject in each sentence. Underline the complete predicate.

1. The underground home contained large, comfortable rooms.

2. The playful child rolled his clay into a ball.

SIMPLE AND COMPLETE SUBJECTS AND PREDICATES

A. Read each sentence. Circle the complete subject. Underline the simple subject.

1. My whole family had a picnic on Saturday.

2. The warm, sunny day was perfect for an outing in the park.

3. My cousin Fred brought his guitar and harmonica.

4. Everyone sang favorite folk songs.

5. The people in the park applauded us.

B. Read each sentence. Circle the complete predicate. Underline the simple predicate.

1. We watched the space shuttle on TV this morning.

2. The huge spaceship rocketed into space at 6:00 A.M.

3. During the flight, the six astronauts released a satellite into space.

4. The space shuttle circled Earth for three days.

5. The spacecraft landed smoothly on Monday at noon.

C. Write three sentences. Circle the complete subject and underline the complete predicate in each sentence.

1. _____

2. _____

3. _____

SIMPLE AND COMPLETE SUBJECTS AND PREDICATES

What part of each sentence is underlined? Fill in the bubble next to the correct answer.

1. <u>My cousin</u> lives on a big ranch in Montana.
   - (a) simple subject
   - (b) complete subject
   - (c) simple predicate

2. Her family <u>raises cattle on the ranch.</u>
   - (a) complete subject
   - (b) simple predicate
   - (c) complete predicate

3. Rosa's <u>job</u> is feeding the chickens before school.
   - (a) simple subject
   - (b) complete subject
   - (c) simple predicate

4. Her brother John <u>feeds the horses.</u>
   - (a) complete subject
   - (b) simple predicate
   - (c) complete predicate

5. <u>My cousin Rosa</u> rides her horse across the range.
   - (a) simple subject
   - (b) complete subject
   - (c) complete predicate

6. John <u>spreads</u> fresh hay in the pasture.
   - (a) simple subject
   - (b) simple predicate
   - (c) complete predicate

7. Their nearest <u>neighbors</u> often go into town with them.
   - (a) simple subject
   - (b) complete subject
   - (c) simple predicate

8. The dinner bell <u>rings</u> at 6:30 every evening.
   - (a) simple subject
   - (b) complete subject
   - (c) simple predicate

9. <u>The whole family</u> sits on the porch and reads about space.
   - (a) simple subject
   - (b) complete subject
   - (c) complete predicate

10. Rosa <u>searches the Internet for sites about animals.</u>
    - (a) complete subject
    - (b) simple predicate
    - (c) complete predicate

COMPOUND SUBJECTS AND PREDICATES

A. Underline the compound subject in each sentence.

1. Pig One, Pig Two, and Pig Three wrote Goldilocks a letter.

2. The bears, rabbits, and pigs attended a party.

3. Carrots, beets, and squash grow in the garden.

4. Later this month Teddy and Osito will visit Baby Bear.

5. My brothers and sisters really enjoyed the housewarming.

B. Circle the compound predicate in each sentence.

1. Peter's mother cleaned and peeled the crispy carrots.

2. The guests laughed and giggled at June's funny jokes.

3. The sly wolves waited and watched for the passing animals.

4. Goldilocks weeds and waters her garden every day.

5. The author writes and edits her amusing fairy tales.

C. Write the compound subject or compound predicate that completes each sentence. Then write *CS* for compound subject or *CP* for compound predicate.

> authors and illustrators   buys and reads

1. My friend _____ all of that author's books. _____

2. Many _____ visit our school. _____

COMPOUND SUBJECTS AND PREDICATES

RETEACHING: A **compound subject** is two or more subjects in the same sentence, usually joined by a connecting word such as *and* or *or*. A **compound predicate** is two or more verbs in the same sentence, usually joined by a connecting word such as *and* or *or*.

A. Underline the simple subject in each sentence. Then rewrite the two sentences as one sentence with a compound subject.

1. The teacher visited the ocean. Her students visited the ocean.

_____

2. Seagulls flew overhead. Pelicans flew overhead.

_____

3. Seashells littered the sand. Seaweed littered the sand.

_____

4. Carlos ran on the beach. Tanya ran on the beach.

_____

B. Circle the simple predicate in each sentence. Then rewrite the two sentences as one sentence with a compound predicate.

1. The artist paints sea life. The artist draws sea life.

_____

2. I collect driftwood. I decorate driftwood.

_____

3. Seals swim near the pier. Seals dive near the pier.

_____

COMPOUND SUBJECTS AND PREDICATES

A. Fill in the bubble next to the compound subject.

1. The deer and bison grazed in the high mountain meadow.
   - (a) deer and bison
   - (b) grazed in
   - (c) high mountain meadow

2. Last weekend Rosa and Kay camped by the lake.
   - (a) Last weekend
   - (b) Rosa and Kay
   - (c) camped by

3. On Friday Alice and I saw a movie about gray wolves.
   - (a) Alice and I
   - (b) saw a movie
   - (c) about gray wolves

4. Last year students and teachers created a wildlife mural.
   - (a) Last year
   - (b) wildlife mural
   - (c) students and teachers

5. My friends and I were hiking in the White Mountains.
   - (a) were hiking
   - (b) friends and I
   - (c) the White Mountains

B. Fill in the bubble next to the compound predicate.

1. All night long the chilly wind moaned and howled.
   - (a) All night long
   - (b) chilly wind
   - (c) moaned and howled

2. Joan picked and peeled the apples in the morning.
   - (a) picked and peeled
   - (b) the apples
   - (c) in the morning

3. Last night Ed and Cody washed and dried the dishes.
   - (a) Last night
   - (b) Ed and Cody
   - (c) washed and dried

4. Many students wrote and revised their book reports.
   - (a) Many students
   - (b) wrote and revised
   - (c) their book reports

5. The famous sculptor cut and polished the cold, gray granite.
   - (a) famous sculptor
   - (b) cut and polished
   - (c) cold, gray granite

COMPOUND SENTENCES

A. Read each sentence. Decide if it is a simple sentence or a compound sentence. Write *simple* **or** *compound* **on the line.**

1. Dad had been horseback riding before. _____

2. Lizzie felt a little nervous on a horse, but he would never admit it. _____

3. He discovered that riding was a lot of fun, and he couldn't wait to tell his friends about it. _____

4. There don't seem to be many bears in the national park this year. _____

5. Suddenly Mom pointed out the car window toward some trees. _____

6. We all looked out the window, but the bears turned out to be people in brown coats. _____

B. Underline the simple sentences that make up each compound sentence.

1. Connor had seen many parks in his life, but he never had seen a park like this one.

2. Dad brought a pair of binoculars, and Nate used them to look for animals.

3. He saw his first live bear, and the hair stood up on his arms.

4. It was an exciting moment, but it only lasted a second.

5. The bear was no bear at all, and Felicia was embarrassed.

6. He hadn't seen a bear, but he kept looking.

COMPOUND SENTENCES

A. Read each sentence. Underline the simple sentences that make up the compound sentence. Circle the coordinating conjunction in each sentence.

1. One day we were in the park, and we saw two ducks swimming by.

2. We watched the ducks for a while, but they disappeared into the tall grass.

3. The ducks might have gone to a nest, or they could have swum to the shore.

4. We walked along the grassy bank, but we could not find them anywhere.

5. We sat down on the dock, and out came the ducks again.

6. One adult duck led six ducklings around the pond, and the other adult followed behind the babies.

B. Read each compound sentence. Choose the coordinating conjunction that makes sense and write it on the line.

1. The ducklings are brown, _____ the adult ducks are white. (but, or)

2. The ducklings were playing, _____ they were learning, too. (but, or)

3. The ducklings ate a lot, _____ they grew quickly. (but, and)

4. We brought bread with us, _____ we fed the ducks. (and, but)

5. Maybe they knew us, _____ maybe they just liked the food we fed them. (and, or)

C. Write a compound sentence. Underline the simple sentences, and circle the coordinating conjunction you used.

_____

_____

COMPOUND SENTENCES

A. Fill in the bubble that tells whether the sentence is a simple sentence or a compound sentence.

1. There are eight planets in our solar system, but there is only one sun.
   - ⓐ simple
   - ⓑ compound

2. The sun is a star, and a star is a giant ball of burning gases.
   - ⓐ simple
   - ⓑ compound

3. A moon is a satellite that moves around a planet.
   - ⓐ simple
   - ⓑ compound

4. Earth has only one moon, but the planet Mars has two moons.
   - ⓐ simple
   - ⓑ compound

5. The word *orbit* means "to travel around something."
   - ⓐ simple
   - ⓑ compound

B. Is the underlined part correct? Fill in the bubble next to the right answer.

1. The sun is <u>a star, but It is not</u> the biggest star.
   - ⓐ a star, but it is not
   - ⓑ a star but, it is not
   - ⓒ correct as is

2. Some stars are bigger than <u>the sun and, some stars</u> are smaller.
   - ⓐ the sun and some stars
   - ⓑ the sun, and some stars
   - ⓒ correct as is

3. Other stars seem smaller than <u>the sun, they are</u> just farther away.
   - ⓐ the sun, but they are
   - ⓑ the sun, They are
   - ⓒ correct as is

4. Do hot stars give off <u>blue light or do they</u> give off red light?
   - ⓐ blue light or, do they
   - ⓑ blue light, or do they
   - ⓒ correct as is

5. Our sun is not the <u>hottest star, but it</u> is not the coolest star either.
   - ⓐ hottest star but it
   - ⓑ hottest star but, it
   - ⓒ correct as is

COMMON AND PROPER NOUNS

A. Circle the common nouns in each sentence.

1. The farmer lives in the green house down the road.

2. The farmer grows wheat, soybeans, and corn.

3. The fields are plowed before he plants the crop.

4. Crops are planted in rows so that they can be watered easily.

5. As the plants grow, the farmer removes weeds and looks for bugs.

B. Underline the proper nouns in each sentence.

1. John Vasquez grows soybeans and alfalfa on a 30-acre farm near Tulsa, Oklahoma.

2. The Vasquez Farm is next to the Rising J Horse Ranch.

3. Mr. Vasquez and his daughter Sally sell alfalfa to the owner of the ranch.

4. Sometimes Joker, a quarter horse, knocks down the fence to get the alfalfa.

5. Every October people come to the Vasquez Farm for the annual Harvest Celebration.

C. Rewrite each sentence. Replace each underlined common noun with a proper noun.

1. We walked down the street to the park.

_____

2. My aunt lives in the city.

_____

COMMON AND PROPER NOUNS

A. Circle the common nouns in each sentence. Underline the proper nouns.

1. The *Atlanta Constitution* published a story about celebrations.

2. *Three Dogs on a Summer Night* is a movie about poodles.

3. We like to sing "She'll Be Comin' 'Round the Mountain" at the campfire.

4. Last August my friend John went to Germany with his grandparents.

5. My family always goes to the beach for Memorial Day.

B. Complete the chart below by writing each common and proper noun in the correct column. Then add three common nouns and three proper nouns to the chart.

newspaper	The Sun News
city	Cobblestone
day	book
magazine	month
Chicago	July
park	Tuesday
Young Arthur	
Yellowstone National Park	

Common Nouns	Proper Nouns
newspaper	*The Sun News*

Name

COMMON AND PROPER NOUNS

Read each sentence. Are the nouns underlined written correctly?
Fill in the bubble next to the right answer.

1. I go to <u>abraham lincoln school</u>.

   ⓐ abraham lincoln School
   ⓑ Abraham Lincoln School
   ⓒ correct as is

2. I brought <u>a peanut butter sandwich</u>.

   ⓐ a Peanut Butter sandwich
   ⓑ a peanut butter Sandwich
   ⓒ correct as is

3. I sang <u>row, row, row your boat</u> today.

   ⓐ Row, Row, Row Your Boat today.
   ⓑ "Row, Row, Row Your Boat" today.
   ⓒ correct as is

4. My school is located on the <u>corner of Maple Avenue and Elm Street</u>.

   ⓐ Corner of Maple Avenue and Elm Street
   ⓑ corner of Maple avenue and Elm street
   ⓒ correct as is

5. I wrote a book report on *cherokee summer* for reading class.

   ⓐ *Cherokee Summer*
   ⓑ *Cherokee summer*
   ⓒ correct as is

6. <u>My best friend John</u> sits in the third row.

   ⓐ My Best Friend John
   ⓑ My best Friend John
   ⓒ correct as is

7. My <u>spanish class begins at noon</u>.

   ⓐ Spanish class begins at Noon
   ⓑ Spanish class begins at noon
   ⓒ correct as is

8. That painting <u>is called "Sunflowers."</u>

   ⓐ is Called sunflowers.
   ⓑ is called Sunflowers.
   ⓒ correct as is

9. I wrote <u>about washington, d.c.</u>

   ⓐ about Washington, D.C.
   ⓑ about Washington, d.c.
   ⓒ correct as is

10. Later I'll go to <u>austin's better books</u>.

    ⓐ Austin's Better Books
    ⓑ austin's Better Books
    ⓒ correct as is

SINGULAR AND PLURAL NOUNS

RETEACHING: A **singular noun** names one person, place, thing, or idea. A **plural noun** names more than one person, place, thing, or idea. Add –s to form the plural of most nouns. Some plural nouns are irregular, and their spellings need to be memorized.

A. Underline the singular nouns in each sentence.

1. I opened the door and found the shoes, cap, and bat I needed for the game.

2. I headed down to the fields with my bat on my shoulder.

3. My friends were standing by the fence near the dugout.

4. We were playing on the same team.

5. That day I hit two grounders, a foul, and a homer.

B. Underline the plural nouns in each sentence.

1. My uncles taught me to stand with my feet closer together.

2. The first time I hit a home run, I danced on each of the bases.

3. In the third game, all the players hit the ball.

4. My brothers, sisters, and cousins came to every game.

5. Four teams were in the playoffs, but our team won the championship.

C. Circle the singular nouns in each sentence. Underline the plural nouns.

1. The teams and players received awards when the season ended.

2. In the games to come, I will try to be a better hitter, catcher, and teammate.

3. My mother and father were the proudest parents at the assembly.

4. They gave me a new glove for my achievements.

SINGULAR AND PLURAL NOUNS

A. Circle the singular nouns in each sentence. Underline the plural nouns in each sentence.

1. My homework last night was to write a story about friends.

2. At home I thought about the people who are my friends.

3. My three dogs, one cat, and four birds are also my pals.

4. I wrote about adventures with my pets and my buddies.

5. My teacher liked my story so much that he read it to his classes.

B. Write each noun in the box in the correct column on the chart. Remember that some nouns keep the same form in the singular and plural.

chair	mice
mouse	chairs
teeth	tooth
sheep	men
foot	feet
man	

	Singular Nouns	Plural Nouns
1.	_____	_____
2.	_____	_____
3.	_____	_____
4.	_____	_____
5.	_____	_____
6.	_____	

C. Write two sentences. Use one singular noun and one plural noun from the chart in each sentence.

1. _____

2. _____

SINGULAR AND PLURAL NOUNS

Decide if the underlined part of the sentence has an error.
Fill in the bubble next to the correct answer.

1. I read seven <u>chapter in my book</u> last night.

   ⓐ chapter in my books
   ⓑ chapters in my book
   ⓒ correct as is

2. In chapter one, <u>a father and a son</u> went to the mountains.

   ⓐ a fathers and a son
   ⓑ a father and a sons
   ⓒ correct as is

3. They built their campsite under some <u>trees near a creeks</u>.

   ⓐ tree near a creeks
   ⓑ trees near a creek
   ⓒ correct as is

4. The first night the father saw <u>a bear eating nut</u>.

   ⓐ a bear eating nuts
   ⓑ a bears eating nuts
   ⓒ correct as is

5. Two <u>bear cubs</u> were in the bushes hiding.

   ⓐ bear cub
   ⓑ bears cub
   ⓒ correct as is

6. The <u>bear cubs' mother</u> helped them find berries to eat.

   ⓐ bear cub's mother
   ⓑ bear cubs mother
   ⓒ correct as is

7. In the morning, there were four <u>deers and a sheep</u> nearby.

   ⓐ deers and a sheeps
   ⓑ deer and a sheep
   ⓒ correct as is

8. The <u>son's teeths</u> were red after eating berries.

   ⓐ son's teeth
   ⓑ son's tooths
   ⓒ correct as is

9. A bird flew <u>by Dads head</u> and into the tent.

   ⓐ by Dad's head
   ⓑ by Dads' head
   ⓒ correct as is

10. It took almost an hour to get that <u>bird out of the tent's</u>.

    ⓐ birds out of the tents
    ⓑ bird out of the tent
    ⓒ correct as is

SUBJECT AND OBJECT PRONOUNS

A. Read the sentences. Circle the subject pronoun in the second sentence that replaces the underlined word or words.

1. The fourth graders read a book about the rain forest.

   They read a book about the rain forest.

2. Then Ada wrote a poem about a huge Kapok tree.

   Then she wrote a poem about a huge Kapok tree.

3. Juan, Jill, and I painted a mural of rain forest mammals.

   We painted a mural of rain forest mammals.

B. Read the sentences. Draw two lines under the object pronoun in the second sentence that replaces the underlined word or words.

1. Mr. Patel's class sent a fan letter to the author.

   Mr. Patel's class sent a letter to her.

2. Ms. Torres, a rain forest expert, visited the fourth graders last week.

   Ms. Torres, a rain forest expert, visited them last week.

3. She said, "You can find information in the library.

   She said, "You can find it in the library."

C. Circle the subject pronoun and underline the object pronoun in each sentence.

1. I saw you at the library yesterday.

2. You can call me tonight about our class project.

3. Will he make an informative poster for us?

SUBJECT AND OBJECT PRONOUNS

A. Choose the pronoun in parentheses ( ) that completes each sentence, and write it on the line. Then identify the kind of pronoun in the sentence by writing *S* for *subject* or *O* for *object*.

1. _____ took a boat trip through the Everglades. (We, Us)   _____

2. The boat's captain gave _____ a special tour. (we, us)   _____

3. The captain said, " _____ will love the wildlife here!" (You, Us)   _____

4. _____ brought a camera in my backpack. (I, Me)   _____

5. I used _____ to photograph birds, turtles, and alligators. (he, it)   _____

6. My sister Kit carried paper and pencils with _____. (she, her)   _____

7. Kit used _____ to sketch scenes of the Everglades. (they, them)   _____

8. _____ is an excellent artist. (She, Her)   _____

B. Rewrite each sentence. Replace the underlined words with the correct subject or object pronoun.

1. <u>Our grandparents</u> sent a postcard to <u>my sister, my brother, and me</u>.

_____

2. <u>The postcard</u> was addressed to <u>my older brother</u>.

_____

C. Write two sentences. In the first, use a subject pronoun. In the second, use an object pronoun.

1. _____

2. _____

SUBJECT AND OBJECT PRONOUNS

A. Fill in the bubble next to the
   pronoun that can replace the
   underlined words.

1. Carlos and Sue have a very popular
   pet-care service.

   ⓐ They
   ⓑ Them
   ⓒ He

2. Many people hire Carlos and Sue to
   feed their cats.

   ⓐ her
   ⓑ they
   ⓒ them

3. Carlos asked Jenna and me to help out
   for a day.

   ⓐ we
   ⓑ us
   ⓒ me

4. Jenna and I were delighted to help.

   ⓐ We
   ⓑ Us
   ⓒ They

5. I agreed to meet Sue at the Chan's
   house this afternoon.

   ⓐ she
   ⓑ her
   ⓒ them

B. Fill in the bubble next to the
   pronoun that correctly
   completes each sentence.

1. Dot, Ed, and _____ visited the Air and
   Space Museum recently.

   ⓐ I
   ⓑ me
   ⓒ us

2. Fortunately, _____ knew his way
   around the huge exhibition hall.

   ⓐ her
   ⓑ he
   ⓒ him

3. _____ really wanted to see the biplanes.

   ⓐ She
   ⓑ Them
   ⓒ Her

4. Then Ed told Dot and _____ about the
   Wright Brothers' flight.

   ⓐ I
   ⓑ me
   ⓒ she

5. I persuaded Dot and _____ to visit the
   museum again soon.

   ⓐ he
   ⓑ him
   ⓒ we

POSSESSIVE PRONOUNS

A. **Underline the possessive pronoun in each sentence.**

1. I miss my best friend, Carlos, because he is spending the summer in Seattle, Washington.

2. He is staying with his favorite cousins, Blanca and Eduardo, during July and August.

3. The cousins have been showing Carlos around their city.

4. When I opened my e-mail this morning, I read about the ferry ride they took across Puget Sound.

5. Blanca also showed Carlos her favorite beach for clam digging.

6. Eduardo said, "Carlos, this will be your best vacation ever!"

7. Then Blanca added, "Our next stop will be the Space Needle."

B. **Write the possessive pronoun from the box that completes each sentence. Use the underlined word or words to help you.**

my	her	his	their	our

1. _____ grandparents sent <u>me</u> a long letter in Spanish.

2. <u>They</u> said that _____ goal was to help me learn the language.

3. <u>Grandmother</u> included the words to _____ favorite Spanish song.

4. <u>Grandfather</u> wrote a list of _____ special tips for learning a language.

5. During _____ next visit, <u>we</u> will try to speak as much Spanish as possible.

6. <u>I</u> know that _____ speaking ability will improve with this kind of help.

POSSESSIVE PRONOUNS

A. Write the possessive pronoun in parentheses ( )
   that correctly completes each sentence.

1. The sports magazine and newspaper are _____. (my, mine)

2. Where is _____ atlas of the United States? (your, yours)

3. Which of the mysteries on the shelf is _____? (your, yours)

4. These new dictionaries will soon be _____. (our, ours)

5. Where is _____ copy of *Charlotte's Web*? (her, hers)

B. Write the possessive pronoun that completes each sentence.

1. My brother and I really enjoy visiting _____ neighborhood library.

2. Every year Ms. Lee, the librarian, displays _____ choices for the year's best reading.

3. Then all the library users vote for _____ favorite books, too.

4. For _____ favorite, I chose a photo biography about Babe Ruth.

5. Luke said that _____ first choice was Jerry Spinelli's new novel.

6. _____ friends Sue and Ed told me that they voted for the same book.

7. I asked them, "What is _____ reason for choosing this book?"

8. They replied, "It's because _____ taste in books is the best."

C. Write three sentences about something you treasure.
   Use a possessive pronoun in each sentence.

1. _____

2. _____

3. _____

POSSESSIVE PRONOUNS

Look at the underlined words in each sentence. Fill in the bubble next to the possessive pronoun that refers back to the underlined word or words.

1. I love baseball, and _____ hobby is collecting baseball cards.

   ⓐ his ⓒ your
   ⓑ our ⓓ my

2. Many baseball-card collectors buy _____ cards from special dealers.

   ⓐ your ⓒ their
   ⓑ his ⓓ her

3. A classmate named Ralph keeps _____ cards in an album.

   ⓐ my ⓒ our
   ⓑ his ⓓ your

4. Sue treasures that rare Jackie Robinson card of _____.

   ⓐ ours ⓒ hers
   ⓑ mine ⓓ his

5. On Saturday Mom and I packed _____ lunch and ate it at the ballpark.

   ⓐ his ⓒ your
   ⓑ their ⓓ our

6. Once all the players signed _____ names on a baseball for me.

   ⓐ his ⓒ my
   ⓑ their ⓓ her

7. "I exclaimed, "This signed baseball is _____ greatest treasure!"

   ⓐ theirs ⓒ ours
   ⓑ my ⓓ yours

8. Grandfather asked me whether this new baseball cap was _____.

   ⓐ her ⓒ you
   ⓑ your ⓓ mine

9. When the players scored, people in the audience waved _____ baseball caps.

   ⓐ his ⓒ their
   ⓑ my ⓓ her

10. I just read a book about Roberto Clemente and _____ amazing career.

    ⓐ his ⓒ their
    ⓑ my ⓓ your

ACTION VERBS

A. Underline the action verb in each sentence, and then write it on the line.

1. Judy Hindley wrote a book about the history of string. _____

2. An illustrator painted funny pictures about string. _____

3. Long ago people twisted vines into long, strong ropes. _____

4. People still weave long, thin fibers into cloth. _____

5. My sister knits sweaters from thick wool yarn. _____

6. We stretched the rope hammock from tree to tree. _____

7. I always tie a ribbon around a birthday package. _____

8. We learned about different kinds of knots. _____

9. He made a belt from three different colors of string. _____

10. We wished for another book by Judy Hindley. _____

B. Underline the action verb that is more vivid.

1. The rabbit quickly (moved, hopped) across the lawn.

2. I (pounded, touched) the nail with my hammer.

3. The thirsty dog (drank, slurped) the water noisily.

4. I (made, sewed) a quilt from scraps of fabric.

C. Write two sentences about how someone did something. Include a vivid action verb in each sentence.

1. _____

2. _____

ACTION VERBS

RETEACHING: An **action verb** is a word that shows action. Some action verbs name actions you can see, such as *jump*. Others name actions you can't see, such as *think*.

A. Circle the action verb in each sentence.

1. People use string in many different ways.

2. Fran and I tie the packages with string.

3. We imagine people from earlier times.

4. These people invented rope, string, and cord.

5. The lively, happy tone of this story amazes me.

B. For each sentence, underline the action verb in parentheses that creates a more vivid picture.

6. We (sit, lounge) on the big chairs near the pool.

7. The horses (go, gallop) across the field.

8. Minna and Max (gulp, eat) their sandwiches in a hurry.

9. The workers (drag, move) the heavy load across the yard.

10. Rosa and I (put, staple) the parts together.

 Use each of these action verbs in a sentence: *follow*, *shout*, *rush*, *slip*, *pound*. Write your sentences on another sheet of paper.

ACTION VERBS

A. Fill in the bubble next to the action verb in each sentence.

1. The space shuttle circled the Earth twenty times.
   - ⓐ space
   - ⓑ circled
   - ⓒ twenty

2. Yesterday morning my class watched the newscast.
   - ⓐ morning
   - ⓑ class
   - ⓒ watched

3. I think about space exploration all the time.
   - ⓐ think
   - ⓑ exploration
   - ⓒ time

4. Before a mission, astronauts train for months.
   - ⓐ mission
   - ⓑ train
   - ⓒ months

5. She read a biography about the first woman in space.
   - ⓐ read
   - ⓑ about
   - ⓒ space

B. For each sentence, fill in the bubble next to the more vivid action verb.

1. At the beach, we _____ for pieces of driftwood.
   - ⓐ looked
   - ⓑ hunted

2. We _____ into the foamy waves.
   - ⓐ walked
   - ⓑ plunged

3. Several artists _____ a huge castle out of sand.
   - ⓐ sculpted
   - ⓑ made

4. I _____ my beach towel under a large umbrella.
   - ⓐ put
   - ⓑ spread

5. The wild horses _____ along the sandy seashore.
   - ⓐ galloped
   - ⓑ ran

Verb Tenses

A. Write *present* if the underlined word is a present tense verb, *past* if the underlined word is a past tense verb, and *future* if it is future tense.

1. The story of sneakers <u>started</u> with the development of rubber. _____

2. People in Central and South America <u>melted</u> gum from trees. _____

3. On Friday she <u>will celebrate</u> her tenth birthday. _____

4. Rubber <u>protected</u> the wearer's feet. _____

5. Gum <u>acts</u> as an eraser. _____

6. Everyone <u>will carry</u> a small backpack. _____

7. Unfortunately, pure rubber <u>cracks</u> in cold weather. _____

8. Charles Goodyear <u>believed</u> in a solution. _____

9. We <u>will visit</u> two museums. _____

10. Goodyear <u>licenses</u> the process to shoe companies. _____

11. The shoe companies <u>manufactured</u> shoes with rubber soles. _____

B. Look at the sentences with present tense verbs in part A. Then rewrite each one with the past tense form of the verb.

1. _____

2. _____

3. _____

VERB TENSES

A. Underline each subject. Decide whether it is singular or plural. Then circle the present tense verb that correctly completes the sentence, and write it on the line.

RETEACHING: Present tense verbs show action that is happening now or on a regular basis. Present tense verbs agree in number with who or what is doing the action. **Past tense verbs** show action that took place in the past. Most past tense verbs end in -ed. **Future tense verbs** show action that will happen in the future. The future tense is formed with the verb *will*.

1. Anna _____ dark-purple sneakers.   wear   wears

2. The sneakers _____ a squeaky sound on the floor.   make   makes

3. The girl _____ her sister how to tie her sneakers.   teach   teaches

4. Tight sneakers _____ your feet.   hurt   hurts

5. Loose sneakers _____ blisters.   cause   causes

6. Joe _____ his new sneakers under his bed.   place   places

7. Rachel _____ new sneakers before the race.   buy   buys

8. The students _____ comfortable sneakers.   want   wants

B. Look at the present tense verbs in the box. Decide whether they agree in number with a singular or a plural subject. Then write each word in the correct column on the chart. An example is given.

lace	laces
design	designs
reach	reaches
erase	erases

Present-Tense Verbs	
With Most Singular Subjects and *he, she, it*	**With Plural Subjects and** *I, we,* **and** *you*
laces	lace

VERB TENSES

A. Look at the underlined verb or verbs. Fill in the bubble next to the correct tense.

B. Decide if the underlined verbs are correct. Fill in the bubble next to the right answer.

1. Tomorrow we <u>will march</u> in the Independence Day parade.

   ⓐ past
   ⓑ present
   ⓒ future

2. Last week my sister and I <u>sewed</u> our old-fashioned costumes.

   ⓐ past
   ⓑ present
   ⓒ future

3. Many townspeople <u>will dress</u> as Western pioneers.

   ⓐ past
   ⓑ present
   ⓒ future

4. Everyone <u>participates</u> in the celebration.

   ⓐ past
   ⓑ present
   ⓒ future

5. <u>Will</u> local cowhands <u>ride</u> their horses?

   ⓐ past
   ⓑ present
   ⓒ future

1. The parade <u>will began</u> at 10:00 tomorrow morning.

   ⓐ will begin
   ⓑ will begins
   ⓒ correct as is

2. The marching bands <u>will arrive</u> in town this afternoon.

   ⓐ will arrives
   ⓑ will arrived
   ⓒ correct as is

3. One parade float <u>will shows</u> an old-time newspaper office.

   ⓐ will showed
   ⓑ will show
   ⓒ correct as is

4. When <u>will</u> the square dancers <u>performed</u>?

   ⓐ will perform
   ⓑ will performs
   ⓒ correct as is

5. Later we <u>will celebrate</u> with a picnic.

   ⓐ will celebrates
   ⓑ will celebrated
   ⓒ correct as is

MAIN AND HELPING VERBS

A. Read each sentence. Underline the helping verb once and the main verb twice.

> **RETEACHING: Main verbs** show the main action in a sentence. **Helping verbs** help the main verb show tense. Helping verbs, such as *am, is, are, was, were, has, have, had,* or *will*, work with main verbs to tell when an action occurs.

1. What will happen to the doughnuts?

2. Uncle Ulysses has equipped the lunchroom with labor-saving devices.

3. Homer was polishing the metal trimmings.

4. Uncle Ulysses had tinkered with the inside workings.

5. The Ladies' Club was gathering.

6. Homer will handle everything.

7. Mr. Gabby was talking to Homer about his job.

8. A chauffeur had helped a woman out of a black car.

9. Now she is wearing an apron.

10. She will need some nutmeg.

B. In each sentence, circle the main verb and underline the helping verb. Then identify when the action occurs by writing *past, present,* or *future.*

1. The lady had asked for baking powder. _____

2. The rings of batter will drop into the hot fat. _____

3. Homer is learning about the doughnut machine. _____

4. People will enjoy the doughnuts later. _____

5. Everyone has eaten Homer's doughnuts. _____

6. We are taking doughnuts for friends. _____

MAIN AND HELPING VERBS

> **RETEACHING: Main verbs** show the main action in a sentence. **Helping verbs** help the main verb show tense. Helping verbs, such as *am, is, are, was, were, has, have, had,* or *will,* work with main verbs to tell when an action occurs.

A. Read each incomplete sentence. Underline the main verb. Then circle the helping verb that correctly completes the sentence, and write it on the line.

1. Justin _____ cooking seafood stew. (will, was)

2. He _____ added spices and lemon juice. (had, is)

3. Sally and Mick _____ prepared stew before. (will, have)

4. Justin _____ tasting the broth. (is, had)

5. "I _____ add a little more pepper," Justin says. (will, has)

6. His friends _____ just arrived for dinner. (are, have)

B. Underline the main verbs, and write the helping verbs on the lines.

1. On Saturday Betty will bake rye bread.   _____

2. Henry has pickled some fresh cucumbers.   _____

3. Gertrude is picking raspberries and blackberries. _____

4. Alison had planted an herb garden.   _____

5. Marie and Harry have tossed the salad.   _____

6. They are planning another picnic.   _____

C. Write sentences using the main and helping verbs below.

1. will meet _____

2. had arrived _____

3. is listening _____

Name

MAIN AND HELPING VERBS

Decide if the underlined verbs in each sentence are correct.
Then fill in the bubble next to the correct answer.

1. Today Francesca <u>will traveled</u> to Peru by plane.

   ⓐ is traveling
   ⓑ am traveling
   ⓒ correct as is

2. She <u>is photograph</u> the stone ruins of Machu Picchu next week.

   ⓐ will photograph
   ⓑ had photographed
   ⓒ correct as is

3. An American explorer <u>had discovered</u> the ancient Incan city in 1911.

   ⓐ has discovered
   ⓑ is discovering
   ⓒ correct as is

4. Since then, many people <u>will visited</u> the ruins of the city.

   ⓐ have visited
   ⓑ have visiting
   ⓒ correct as is

5. Yesterday Francesca's brothers <u>had looking</u> at pictures of Machu Picchu.

   ⓐ have looking
   ⓑ were looking
   ⓒ correct as is

6. They <u>were wondering</u> about the Incan civilization.

   ⓐ had wondering
   ⓑ has wonder
   ⓒ correct as is

7. Centuries ago the Inca <u>had creating</u> a great empire.

   ⓐ have creating
   ⓑ had created
   ⓒ correct as is

8. What <u>had happening</u> to them?

   ⓐ has happening
   ⓑ had happened
   ⓒ correct as is

9. The Spanish explorers <u>will conquered</u> the Inca in 1532.

   ⓐ had conquered
   ⓑ are conquered
   ⓒ correct as is

10. Francesca <u>will discover</u> Incan culture in present-day Peru.

   ⓐ has discovering
   ⓑ was discover
   ⓒ correct as is

LINKING VERBS

A. Underline the linking verb in each sentence, and circle the words it links.

1. I am an enthusiastic reader.

2. My favorite books are nonfiction.

3. This bookstore is the best one in town.

4. The nonfiction books here are always interesting.

5. The store's owner is very knowledgeable.

6. His name is Terry Baldes.

7. Mr. Baldes was once an inventor and a scientist.

8. The bookstore's windows were very attractive last month.

9. Last Saturday's main event was an appearance by my favorite author.

10. My friends are big admirers of Mr. Baldes.

B. Write the linking verb in each sentence on the line.

1. An important invention is the telephone. _____

2. The telephone's inventor was Alexander Graham Bell. _____

3. At one time, most telephones were black. _____

4. Today cellular phones are very popular. _____

5. Cell phones were uncommon 25 years ago. _____

C. Write two sentences. Include a linking verb in each one.

1. _____

2. _____

Name _____

LINKING VERBS

RETEACHING: A **linking verb** links the subject of a sentence to other words in the sentence. A linking verb does not show action. It tells what the subject is, was, or will be.

A. Underline the correct linking verb in ( ). Write *S* if the subject is singular and *P* if it is plural.

1. The natural history museum (was, were) very busy last weekend. _____

2. Many visitors (was, were) tourists. _____

3. The new displays of rocks and gems (is, are) very popular. _____

4. One amazing rock (is, are) bright blue. _____

5. My favorite gems (was, were) the purple amethysts. _____

6. The gold nuggets (is, are) bright yellow. _____

7. The museum's first floor (is, are) full of Native American artifacts. _____

8. The carved wooden canoes (is, are) enormous. _____

9. The Tlingit woodcarvers (was, were) true artists. _____

10. This canoe (was, were) hand painted over a hundred years ago. _____

11. I (am, is) a big supporter of the museum. _____

B. Complete each sentence. Write *is* or *are* on the line.

1. The apatasaurus skeleton _____ gigantic.

2. These saber-tooth tigers _____ very impressive.

3. The exhibit cards _____ most informative.

4. The tiny dinosaur _____ really cute.

C. Write a sentence with a singular subject and a sentence with a plural subject. Include a linking verb in each sentence.

1. _____

2. _____

LINKING VERBS

Read each incomplete sentence below. Then fill in the bubble next to the linking verb that correctly completes the sentence.

1. Denver, Colorado, _____ a large city.
   - (a) were
   - (b) are
   - (c) is

2. This growing metropolis _____ a mile high.
   - (a) are
   - (b) is
   - (c) were

3. Gold prospectors _____ the city's founders in 1858.
   - (a) is
   - (b) was
   - (c) were

4. From 1860 to 1945, Denver _____ a mining and agricultural community.
   - (a) were
   - (b) was
   - (c) will be

5. Today many local residents _____ government workers.
   - (a) are
   - (b) is
   - (c) was

6. Now the automobile _____ a quick way to travel.
   - (a) were
   - (b) is
   - (c) are

7. In earlier times, horses and buggies _____ popular modes of transportation.
   - (a) were
   - (b) is
   - (c) was

8. I _____ a student in a Denver public school.
   - (a) were
   - (b) am
   - (c) is

9. Last year my school's sports teams _____ very successful.
   - (a) was
   - (b) were
   - (c) is

10. I _____ a spectator at the local games.
    - (a) was
    - (b) were
    - (c) is

IRREGULAR VERBS

A. Underline the irregular verb in each sentence.

1. This morning Mom bought red and green toothbrushes.

2. Pat made a tuna sandwich in the kitchen.

3. Mom quickly came into the dining room.

4. Deever rode her bicycle over to Pat's house.

5. Deever shook her head in great amusement.

6. They heard a great deal of noise in the kitchen.

7. Deever took a close look at the bright red toothbrush.

8. Pat carefully thought about the green and red toothbrushes.

9. Deever broke the silence with a sly laugh.

B. Circle the irregular past tense verb in parentheses ( ). Then write it on the line to complete the sentence.

1. We _____ a funny story about two toothbrushes. (hear, heard)

2. Pat _____ his decision after fifteen long minutes. (made, make)

3. Mom finally _____ E.J. an orange toothbrush. (buy, bought)

4. E.J. _____ into a song with a big smile on his face. (broke, break)

5. We all _____ to the nearest supermarket on our bikes. (ride, rode)

6. Deever _____ to the store with us. (came, come)

7. E.J. _____ with laughter at Pat's joke. (shook, shake)

IRREGULAR VERBS

A. Underline the helping verb and the irregular past participle in each sentence.

1. We have chosen a fantastic day for our school picnic.

2. Mr. Torres has brought all the food and beverages in his van.

3. We have eaten all of the carrots on the table.

4. Ms. Chang has hidden the prizes for the treasure hunt.

5. By noon our teacher had taken over forty photographs.

6. All the fourth graders have gone on a short walk to the lake.

7. They had heard about the great paddleboats there.

8. Some of my friends have ridden in the boats.

9. The school has bought new sports equipment for our afternoon game.

B. Circle the irregular past participle in parentheses ( ). Then write it on the line to complete the sentence.

1. By May I had _____ about an amazing automobile. (hear, heard)

2. Test drivers have _____ it on experimental runs. (taken, took)

3. My friend's family has _____ to Utah to see it. (went, gone)

4. My friend has _____ in the automobile, too. (ridden, rode)

5. I have _____ this car as a research topic. (chose, chosen)

6. My mom has _____ photos of the car, too. (bought, buy)

7. I have also _____ home articles and books about the car. (bring, brought)

IRREGULAR VERBS

A. Complete each sentence. Fill in the bubble next to the irregular past-tense verb.

1. Last week, we _____ the news about our baseball team's victory.

    ⓐ hear
    ⓑ heard
    ⓒ hears

2. Yesterday morning, Mom and I _____ the bus downtown.

    ⓐ rode
    ⓑ rides
    ⓒ ride

3. Then we _____ in line for an hour.

    ⓐ stand
    ⓑ stands
    ⓒ stood

4. We finally _____ four tickets to the first game in the playoffs.

    ⓐ bought
    ⓑ buys
    ⓒ buying

5. Then we _____ lunch to celebrate.

    ⓐ eat
    ⓑ ate
    ⓒ eats

B. Complete each sentence. Fill in the bubble next to the correct helping verb and past participle.

1. That old adobe house _____ on top of the mesa for a century.

    ⓐ has stood
    ⓑ has stand
    ⓒ has stands

2. We _____ up there many times.

    ⓐ have rode
    ⓑ have ride
    ⓒ have ridden

3. Our great-grandfather _____ pictures of the house long ago.

    ⓐ had drawn
    ⓑ had draw
    ⓒ had drew

4. We _____ the sketches for many years.

    ⓐ have keep
    ⓑ have kept
    ⓒ have keeps

5. Fortunately, my family _____ very good care of the drawings.

    ⓐ has took
    ⓑ has take
    ⓒ has taken

ADJECTIVES

A. In the following sentences, circle the adjectives that tell what kind. Underline the adjectives that tell how many.

1. We watched many colorful creatures swim through the dark water.

2. A few tilefish were building small burrows.

3. Suddenly one strange and unusual fish swam by us.

4. Eugenie swam over to the mysterious fish.

5. It looked like a jawfish with a big head and four dark patches on its back.

6. Was this rare fish a new species?

7. We put the tiny fish in a large bucket of cold seawater.

8. Eugenie has made several amazing discoveries.

B. Complete each sentence with an adjective that tells what kind or how many.

1. The _____ fish was named after David.

2. The fish had a _____ head.

3. The fish lived in a _____ burrow at the bottom of the ocean.

4. The tiny fish turned out to be a _____ species.

5. David took _____ photographs that appeared in magazines.

C. Write two sentences. Use adjectives that tell what kind and how many in each sentence.

1. _____

2. _____

ADJECTIVES

A. Write an adjective to complete each sentence.

1. The _____ dog ate most of the cat's food.

2. The _____ cat found a nearly empty bowl.

3. The cat ate what remained of her _____ meal.

4. The cat pushed the _____ dish over to where a _____ girl was sitting.

5. The girl refilled the dish with _____ food.

B. Read each sentence. Circle the adjective that describes each underlined noun.

1. The gray <u>cat</u> saw the shaggy <u>dog</u> sitting in the dark <u>corner</u>.

2. The cat saw some <u>cat food</u> on the dog's droopy <u>mouth</u>.

3. The cat slipped out of the little <u>kitchen</u> and went into the quiet <u>backyard</u>.

4. She started digging in the soft <u>dirt</u> under a shady <u>tree</u>.

5. The dog looked out the enormous <u>window</u> and saw the cat with a large <u>bone</u>.

C. Write two sentences that tell what happened next. Use vivid adjectives in your writing.

1. _____

_____

2. _____

_____

ADJECTIVES

Fill in the bubble next to the word in each sentence that is an adjective.

1. I had an important decision to make this morning.
   - ⓐ important
   - ⓑ decision
   - ⓒ morning

2. I wanted to buy an appropriate pet for my sister.
   - ⓐ wanted
   - ⓑ buy
   - ⓒ appropriate

3. First, I looked at a striped lizard.
   - ⓐ First
   - ⓑ striped
   - ⓒ lizard

4. Then, I considered getting two hamsters.
   - ⓐ considered
   - ⓑ two
   - ⓒ hamsters

5. The white hamster was named George.
   - ⓐ white
   - ⓑ hamster
   - ⓒ George

6. I admired the noisy parrot.
   - ⓐ I
   - ⓑ noisy
   - ⓒ parrot

7. I watched a gigantic turtle on a rock.
   - ⓐ gigantic
   - ⓑ turtle
   - ⓒ rock

8. Several gerbils ran on a wheel.
   - ⓐ Several
   - ⓑ gerbils
   - ⓒ wheel

9. I finally decided to get a saltwater aquarium.
   - ⓐ decided
   - ⓑ saltwater
   - ⓒ aquarium

10. I'm sure my family will enjoy the colorful fish.
    - ⓐ sure
    - ⓑ family
    - ⓒ colorful

ADJECTIVES THAT COMPARE

RETEACHING: **Comparative adjectives** compare two things by adding –er to the adjective or by using the word *more*. **Superlative adjectives** compare three or more things by adding –est or by using the word *most*.

A. In each sentence, underline the adjective that compares.

1. Anna is older than her brother Caleb.

2. That was the loudest thunderstorm of the entire summer.

3. Seal is the biggest cat that I have ever seen.

4. Papa is quieter than Sarah.

5. The roof of the barn is higher than the top of the haystack.

6. The kitten's fur was softer than lamb's wool.

7. Sarah pointed to the brightest star in the sky.

8. What is the saddest moment in the story?

B. Underline the adjective in parentheses ( ) that completes each sentence correctly. On the line write *two* or *more than two* to show how many things are being compared.

1. On the (hotter, hottest) day in July, we went swimming. _____

2. Today is (warmer, warmest) than last Tuesday. _____

3. Is winter (colder, coldest) on the prairie or by the sea? _____

4. This is the (taller, tallest) tree in the entire state. _____

5. Sarah's hair is (longer, longest) than Maggie's. _____

6. Of the three dogs, Nick was the (friendlier, friendliest). _____

7. Caleb's horse is (younger, youngest) than Anna's pony. _____

8. The new foal is the (livelier, liveliest) animal on the farm. _____

ADJECTIVES THAT COMPARE

Choose the adjective that completes each
sentence and write it on the line.

funnier   funniest

1. The _____ book I've ever read is about a family of mice.

2. The book is much _____ than the movie.

busier   busiest

3. The book department is _____ than the shoe department.

4. The _____ bookstore in the city is on King Street.

more exciting   most exciting

5. Hiking in the woods is _____ than watching TV.

6. This is the _____ ride at the amusement park.

more challenging   most challenging

7. Is a game of checkers _____ than a game of chess?

8. I think that soccer is the _____ of all the field games.

more tiring   most tiring

9. We found that swimming was _____ than walking.

10. Of all the afternoon's activities, tennis was the _____ .

more delicious   most delicious

11. The strawberries are _____ than the green grapes.

12. This is the _____ apple that I have ever eaten.

ADJECTIVES THAT COMPARE

Fill in the bubble next to the correct comparative or superlative adjective.

1. I believe that a dog is much _____ than a cat.

   ⓐ friendlier

   ⓑ friendliest

2. My poodle is the _____ dog of all the dogs in the dog-training class.

   ⓐ more intelligent

   ⓑ most intelligent

3. The gazelle is the _____ animal in the animal park.

   ⓐ more graceful

   ⓑ most graceful

4. The movie about turtles is _____ than the book about frogs.

   ⓐ more fascinating

   ⓑ most fascinating

5. The diamondback rattler is _____ than a bull snake.

   ⓐ more dangerous

   ⓑ most dangerous

6. I think that the jaguar is the _____ of all the big cats.

   ⓐ more beautiful

   ⓑ most beautiful

7. Did you know that a cheetah is _____ than a lion?

   ⓐ swifter

   ⓑ swiftest

8. Your parrot is _____ than my cockatoo.

   ⓐ noisier

   ⓑ noisiest

9. This chimpanzee is _____ than that gorilla.

   ⓐ more playful

   ⓑ most playful

10. That polar bear is the _____ mammal I've ever seen.

    ⓐ larger

    ⓑ largest

PREPOSITIONS

A. Read each sentence. Underline each group of words that begins with a preposition, and circle the preposition. Some sentences have more than one prepositional phrase.

1. The boy cut out pictures of mountains, rivers, and lakes.

2. He enjoyed pasting them on the walls of his room.

3. His father responded to the scenes in the pictures.

4. He decided that he would take his son on a camping trip.

5. They carried supplies in a backpack and knapsack.

6. The boy drank a hot drink from his father's mug.

7. That afternoon they hiked in the mountains for hours.

8. They were disappointed when they found many campers at the Lost Lake.

9. The boy and his father continued on their journey.

10. Finally, they stopped at a quiet place for the night.

11. The boy and his father ate and slept in a tent.

12. The tent kept them safe from the wind and rain.

13. Will this trip make the boy feel closer to his father?

14. What else will they see on their camping trip?

B. Complete each sentence with a prepositional phrase.

1. Let's go to the store _____

2. I just received a letter _____

3. Eduardo found his missing sneaker _____

4. Tanya always plays soccer _____

PREPOSITIONS

A. Circle the preposition in each sentence.

1. Herb often goes hiking in the Rocky Mountains.

2. He always carries a water jug and a compass with him.

3. Today he saw wild columbines growing on the mountainsides.

4. Then he passed a doe and her fawn searching for food.

5. The deer stood very still and stared at him.

6. Then the two creatures disappeared into the woods.

B. Complete each sentence with a prepositional phrase. You may wish to use some of the prepositions from part A or the prepositions *from*, *over*, *under*, *to*, or *by*.

1. Each summer Suzanne goes camping _____

2. Usually they camp _____

3. They pitch their small, green tent _____

4. Her mother cooks _____

5. Suzanne sometimes hears ravens cawing _____

6. Once she saw a black bear running very quickly _____

C. Use the prepositions *of*, *with*, and *at* in three sentences of your own.

1. _____

2. _____

3. _____

PREPOSITIONS

Fill in the bubble next to the word from the sentence that is a preposition.

1. Last summer the Camachos took a trip to three national parks.
   - (a) to
   - (b) trip
   - (c) Last

2. The family was from San Antonio, Texas.
   - (a) family
   - (b) was
   - (c) from

3. The family left their home on a Saturday morning.
   - (a) family
   - (b) on
   - (c) left

4. First they headed for Carlsbad Caverns, New Mexico.
   - (a) for
   - (b) First
   - (c) Caverns

5. Rita saw bats fly over her head.
   - (a) saw
   - (b) bats
   - (c) over

6. Next the family visited cliff dwellings left by the Anasazi people.
   - (a) Next
   - (b) cliff
   - (c) by

7. Then they camped at Arches National Park.
   - (a) at
   - (b) they
   - (c) Then

8. Edwin sat under a sandstone formation called Delicate Arch.
   - (a) sat
   - (b) under
   - (c) called

9. Rita and Edwin took photographs of their favorite sites.
   - (a) took
   - (b) their
   - (c) of

10. They talked with their friends the next week.
    - (a) talked
    - (b) with
    - (c) their

SUBJECT-VERB AGREEMENT

A. Underline the subject once and the verb twice. Write *present* if the verb is in the present tense and *past* if the verb is in the past tense.

1. Tucker lives in a drain pipe. _____

2. It opens into a pocket. _____

3. Tucker collected stuffing for the pocket. _____

4. The mouse filled the pocket with paper and cloth. _____

5. Tucker sits at the opening of the drain pipe. _____

6. He watches the people in the subway station. _____

7. The young boy worked at his father's newsstand. _____

8. They sell papers there on weekdays. _____

B. Underline the subject once and the verb twice. Then write *singular* if the subject and verb are singular and *plural* if the subject and verb are plural.

1. The nighttime crowd passes by quickly. _____

2. Trains run less often at that time. _____

3. Papa waits for business. _____

4. The station feels quiet and lonely. _____

5. People rush home at the end of the day. _____

6. Mama and Papa make very little money. _____

SUBJECT-VERB AGREEMENT

A. Underline the subject. Then circle the verb in parentheses ( ) that agrees with the subject.

RETEACHING: **Subjects** and **verbs** in a sentence must agree in number. Add –s or –es to present tense verbs used with *he, she, it,* or a singular noun. Do not add –s or –es to present tense verbs used with *I, you, we, they,* or a plural noun.

1. Crickets _____ a musical sound.
   (make, makes)

2. Actually, only the males _____ sounds. (produce, produces)

3. I _____ for the sound of crickets on a summer night.
   (listen, listens)

4. You _____ them in places outside the city. (hear, hears)

5. Mario _____ a cricket in the subway station. (find, finds)

6. His mother _____ the cricket a "bug." (call, calls)

B. Underline the subject and verb in each sentence. Then rewrite each sentence in the present tense. Be sure your subjects and verbs agree.

1. Mario wanted the cricket for a pet.

   _____

2. He wished for a pet of his own.

   _____

3. Crickets seemed like unusual pets to his mother.

   _____

4. Maybe insects scared her!

   _____

Name

SUBJECT-VERB AGREEMENT

A. Fill in the bubble next to the verb that agrees with the subject of the sentence.

1. Chester ——— tall buildings for the first time.
   - (a) see
   - (b) sees

2. The city ——— him.
   - (a) surprise
   - (b) surprises

3. The stars ——— Chester's attention.
   - (a) catch
   - (b) catches

4. Maybe he ——— for his home in Connecticut.
   - (a) wish
   - (b) wishes

5. One star ——— familiar to Chester.
   - (a) is
   - (b) are

B. Is the underlined verb correct? Fill in the bubble next to the right answer.

1. Now the animals <u>crouch</u> against the cement.
   - (a) crouches
   - (b) crouched
   - (c) correct as is

2. At this moment, their eyes <u>is</u> on the sky.
   - (a) are
   - (b) were
   - (c) correct as is

3. The sky <u>looks</u> so beautiful right now.
   - (a) look
   - (b) looked
   - (c) correct as is

4. Last night the cricket <u>view</u> Times Square for the first time.
   - (a) views
   - (b) viewed
   - (c) correct as is

5. One week ago, Chester <u>experiences</u> a much different world.
   - (a) experience
   - (b) experienced
   - (c) correct as is

PUNCTUATING DIALOGUE

A. Underline the exact words of the speaker. Circle the quotation marks.

1. Eva exclaimed, "I really like tall tales!"

2. "Davy Crockett is my favorite character," said Juan.

3. I asked, "Who likes Sally Ann Thunder Ann Whirlwind?"

> **RETEACHING: Quotation marks** show the beginning and end of a speaker's exact words. When the speaker comes first, place a comma between it and the beginning quotation mark. When a quotation comes first, use a comma, question mark, or exclamation point before the end quotation mark. Use a period at the end of the sentence.

B. Add the missing quotation marks to each sentence.

1. __I am a big fan of hers,__ replied Shavon.

2. I added, __Sally can even sing a wolf to sleep.__

3. __How did Sally tame King Bear?__ asked our teacher.

4. __Sally really ought to be in the movies,__ said Don.

C. Write the missing punctuation marks in each sentence.

1. __What kind of person is Sally__ __asked Davy Crockett__

2. The schoolmarm replied__ __Sally is a special friend__ __

3. __She can laugh the bark off a pine tree__ __added Lucy__

4. The preacher said__ __She can dance a rock to pieces__ __

5. __I'm very impressed__ __exclaimed Davy__

D. Write two sentences of dialogue between Davy Crockett and Sally.

1. _____

2. _____

PUNCTUATING DIALOGUE

A. Add the missing commas to the sentences.

1. "Well__ we are having a canned-food drive next week."

2. "Oh__ Ed__ can you bring some containers to school?"

3. "Yes__ I have several at home, Jody."

4. "Thank you__ Mr. Poole, for all your suggestions."

B. Add the missing quotation marks and/or commas to each sentence.

1. __Kim, your posters for the talent contest are terrific!__ I exclaimed.

2. She replied, __Thank you, Doug, for your kind words.__

3. Our teacher asked, __Meg__ will you play your guitar or sing?__

4. "Oh__ I plan to do both,__ said Meg.

5. __Will you perform your juggling act this year Roberto?__ Jay asked.

6. __No__ I want to do a comedy routine,__ he replied.

C. Add the missing punctuation to each sentence.

1. __Kit__ which act did you like best__ __ asked Mina__

2. He replied__ __Oh__ I enjoyed the singing pumpkins and the tap dancing elephants__ __

3. __Well__ I liked the guitar player__ __ said Mina__

D. Write two more sentences of dialogue about a school talent show.

1. _____

2. _____

Name _____

PUNCTUATING DIALOGUE

Decide if there is an error in the underlined part of each sentence.
Fill in the bubble next to the correct answer.

1. "Rosa, tell me one of your <u>favorite jokes</u>" said Ken.
   - ⓐ favorite jokes."
   - ⓑ favorite jokes,"
   - ⓒ correct as is

2. "What do <u>sharks eat?</u> she asked.
   - ⓐ sharks eat?"
   - ⓑ sharks eat"
   - ⓒ correct as is

3. <u>Ken replied "tell</u> me. I don't know.
   - ⓐ Ken replied. "Tell
   - ⓑ Ken replied, "Tell
   - ⓒ correct as is

4. "They eat peanut butter and jellyfish <u>sandwiches," replied</u> Rosa.
   - ⓐ sandwiches" replied
   - ⓑ sandwiches." replied
   - ⓒ correct as is

5. <u>Oh, that</u> was funny!" exclaimed Ken.
   - ⓐ "Oh, that
   - ⓑ Oh that
   - ⓒ correct as is

6. <u>"Rosa? tell</u> me another one," he said.
   - ⓐ "Rosa tell
   - ⓑ "Rosa, tell
   - ⓒ correct as is

7. "What years do frogs <u>like best</u> asked Rosa smugly.
   - ⓐ like best?"
   - ⓑ like best,"
   - ⓒ correct as is

8. "Frogs like Hoppy New <u>Years,"</u> <u>laughed</u> Ken.
   - ⓐ Years" laughed
   - ⓑ Years, laughed
   - ⓒ correct as is

9. <u>"No frogs</u> like leap years," insisted Rosa.
   - ⓐ "No, frogs
   - ⓑ No frogs
   - ⓒ correct as is

10. "Ken <u>said. "my</u> joke is funnier."
    - ⓐ said "My
    - ⓑ said, "My
    - ⓒ correct as is

ADVERBS

A. Underline the verb. Then circle the adverb that tells when.

1. Later, newsboys shouted the weekend forecast.

2. Yesterday, a huge snowstorm hit New York City.

3. It got very cold soon.

4. A train tried to plow through the snow earlier.

5. Then the train went off the track.

B. Underline the verb. Then circle the adverb that tells where.

1. Snow fell everywhere.

2. Drifts of snow piled up.

3. People were trapped inside.

4. Some people tunneled out from their homes.

5. People there traveled by sled.

C. Underline the adverb in each sentence. Write _when_ if the adverb tells when or _where_ if it tells where.

1. People had never seen a storm so bad. _____

2. Pipes burst underground. _____

3. The water inside had frozen. _____

4. Soon people started to freeze, too. _____

ADVERBS

A. Underline the verb once. Then circle the adverb that describes the verb and tells how.

1. Grandma talked happily to the frolicking sea lions.

2. The sea birds squawked sharply as they dived.

3. Andy greeted the girl and Grandma warmly.

4. He guided them expertly through the Galápagos Islands.

5. Grandma wrote about the islands regularly in her diary.

6. The girl recorded the trip faithfully in her diary.

7. She responded personally to everything she saw.

8. Andy and the girl looked eagerly at the creatures on the shore.

9. Grandma and the girl jumped quickly off the boat.

10. They snorkeled easily with their breathing tubes and fins.

11. The girl saw sea creatures clearly through her face mask.

12. She gazed intently at the yellow-tailed surgeonfish.

13. Swiftly the sea lions surrounded Grandma and the girl.

14. The sea lion pups chased and nipped one another playfully.

B. Complete each sentence with an action verb and an adverb that describes it and tells how.

1. The big male sea lion _____

2. The girl and her grandmother _____

ADVERBS

A. Fill in the bubble next to the adverb that tells how.

1. Carolina and Gabriella dove rapidly under a big wave.

   (a) rapidly
   (b) under
   (c) big

2. Then a wave crashed loudly against the shore.

   (a) crashed
   (b) loudly
   (c) against

3. Both Carolina and Gabriella were very strong swimmers.

   (a) Both
   (b) very
   (c) strong

4. At the beach, the tide was somewhat low.

   (a) At
   (b) low
   (c) somewhat

5. Carolina quickly spotted a group of bottle-nose dolphins.

   (a) quickly
   (b) spotted
   (c) bottle-nose

B. Fill in the bubble next to the word that is <u>not</u> an adverb.

1. Gabriella and Carolina swam very slowly toward the playful mammals.

   (a) very
   (b) slowly
   (c) playful

2. "They are so curious!" Carolina exclaimed excitedly.

   (a) so
   (b) curious
   (c) excitedly

3. One baby dolphin came very close.

   (a) One
   (b) very
   (c) close

4. The mother dolphin nudged Carolina so gently.

   (a) nudged
   (b) so
   (c) gently

5. Then swiftly and mysteriously, the dolphins disappeared.

   (a) swiftly
   (b) disappeared
   (c) mysteriously

Page 5
A. 1. declarative   4. imperative
   2. interrogative   5. exclamatory
   3. imperative   6. interrogative
B. 1. incomplete   4. incomplete
   2. complete   5. complete
   3. complete
C. 1. Sarah stood at the edge of the square.
   2. The sword slid out of the stone.

Page 6
A. 1. ?, interrogative   3. ., imperative
   2. !, exclamatory   4. ., declarative
B. 1. listened, declarative   3. pass, imperative
   2. play, interrogative   4. won, exclamatory
C. Answers will vary.

Page 7
1. b   3. c   5. c   7. c   9. a
2. b   4. a   6. b   8. a   10. b

Page 8
A. 1. A small family | lived on a faraway planet.
   2. The family's two children | played near the space launch.
   3. The little girl | dreamed about life on Earth.
   4. Huge spaceships | landed daily on the planet.
   5. The spaceship mechanics | repaired huge cargo ships.
   6. Twinkling stars | appeared in the black sky.
B. 1. The planet's inhabitants | lived in underground homes.
   2. A special machine | manufactures air inside the family's home.
   3. The athletic girl | jumped high into the air.
   4. Many toys and games | cluttered the children's playroom.
   5. The children's father | described weather on Earth.
C. 1. (The underground home) contained large, comfortable rooms.
   2. (The playful child) rolled his clay into a ball.

Page 9
A. 1. My whole family   4. Everyone
   2. The warm, sunny day   5. The people in the park
   3. My cousin Fred
B. 1. watched the space shuttle on TV this morning.
   2. rocketed into space at 6:00 A.M.
   3. released a satellite into space.
   4. circled Earth for three days.
   5. landed smoothly on Monday at noon.
C. Answers will vary.

Page 10
1. b   3. a   5. b   7. a   9. b
2. c   4. c   6. b   8. c   10. c

Page 11
A. 1. Pig One, Pig Two, and Pig Three
   2. bears, rabbits, and pigs
   3. Carrots, beets, and squash
   4. Teddy and Osito
   5. brothers and sisters
B. 1. cleaned and peeled   4. weeds and waters
   2. laughed and giggled   5. writes and edits
   3. waited and watched
C. 1. buys and reads, CP
   2. authors and illustrators, CS

Page 12
A. 1. teacher, students; The teacher and her students visited the ocean.
   2. Seagulls, Pelicans; Seagulls and pelicans flew overhead.
   3. Seashells, Seaweed; Seashells and seaweed littered the sand.
   4. Carlos, Tanya; Carlos and Tanya ran on the beach
B. 1. paints, draws; The artist paints and draws sea life.
   2. collect, decorate; I collect and decorate driftwood.
   3. swim, dive; Seals swim and dive near the pier.

Page 13
A. 1. a   2. b   3. a   4. c   5. b
B. 1. c   2. a   3. c   4. b   5. b

Page 14
A. 1. simple   3. compound   5. simple
   2. compound   4. simple   6. compound
B. 1. Connor had seen many parks in his life, but he never had seen a park like this one.
   2. Dad brought a pair of binoculars, and Nate used them to look for animals.
   3. He saw his first live bear, and the hair stood up on his arms.
   4. It was an exciting moment, but it only lasted a second.
   5. The bear was no bear at all, and Felicia was embarrassed.
   6. He hadn't seen a bear, but he kept looking.

Page 15
A. 1. One day we were in the park, (and) we saw two ducks swimming by.
   2. We watched the ducks for a while, (but) they disappeared into the tall grass.
   3. The ducks might have gone to a nest, (or) they could have swum to the shore.
   4. We walked along the grassy bank, (but) we could not find them anywhere.
   5. We sat down on the dock, (and) out came the ducks again.
   6. One adult duck led six ducklings around the pond, (and) the other adult followed behind the babies.
B. 1. but   3. and   5. or
   2. but   4. and
C. Answers will vary.

Page 16
A. 1. b   2. b   3. a   4. b   5. a
B. 1. a   2. b   3. a   4. b   5. c

Page 17
A. 1. farmer, house, road
   2. farmer, wheat, soybeans, corn
   3. fields, crop
   4. crops, rows
   5. plants, farmer, weeds, bugs
B. 1. John Vasquez, Tulsa, Oklahoma
   2. Vasquez Farm, Rising J Horse Ranch
   3. Mr. Vasquez, Sally
   4. Joker
   5. October, Vasquez Farm, Harvest Celebration
C. 1. the street, park
      Sample answer: We walked down Oak Street to Blair Park.
   2. aunt, the city
      Sample answer: My Aunt Ellen lives in Denver.

Page 18
A. 1. (story, celebrations); _Atlanta Constitution_
   2. (movie, poodles); _Three Dogs on a Summer Night_
   3. (campfire); "She'll Be Comin' 'Round the Mountain"
   4. (friend, grandparents); _August, John, Germany_
   5. (family, beach); _Memorial Day_
B. Common nouns: newspaper, city, day, magazine, park, book, month
   Proper nouns: The Sun News, Chicago, Tuesday, Cobblestone, Yellowstone National Park, Young Arthur, July

Page 19
1. b   3. b   5. a   7. b   9. a
2. c   4. c   6. c   8. c   10. a

Page 20
A. 1. door, cap, bat, game   4. team
   2. bat, shoulder   5. day, foul, homer
   3. fence, dugout
B. 1. uncles, feet   4. brothers, sisters, cousins
   2. bases   5. teams, playoffs
   3. players
C. 1. (season); teams, players; awards
   2. (hitter), (catcher) (teammate); games
   3. (mother), (father), (assembly); parents
   4. (glove); achievements

Page 21
A. 1. (homework), (night), (story); friends
   2. (home); people, friends
   3. (cat); dogs, birds, pals
   4. adventures, pets, buddies
   5. (teacher), (story); classes
B. Singular nouns:
   1. chair   3. tooth   5. foot
   2. mouse   4. sheep   6. man
   Plural Nouns:
   1. chairs   3. teeth   5. feet
   2. mice   4. sheep   6. men
C. Answers will vary.

Page 22

1. b 3. b 5. c 7. b 9. a
2. c 4. a 6. c 8. a 10. b

Page 23

A. 1. The fourth graders; (they)
   2. Ada; (she)
   3. Juan, Jill, and I; (We)
B. 1. the author; her
   2. the fourth graders; them
   3. information; it
C. 1. (I), you   2. (You), me   3. (he), us

Page 24

A. 1. We; S   4. I; S   7. them; O
   2. us; O   5. it; O   8. She; S
   3. You; S   6. her; O
B. 1. They sent a postcard to us.
   2. It was addressed to him.
C. Answers will vary.

Page 25

A. 1. a   2. c   3. b   4. a   5. b
B. 1. a   2. b   3. a   4. b   5. b

Page 26

A. 1. my   3. their   5. her   7. Our
   2. his   4. my   6. your
B. 1. My   3. her   5. our
   2. their   4. his   6. my

Page 27

A. 1. mine   3. yours   5. her
   2. your   4. ours
B. 1. our   4. my   7. your
   2. her   5. his   8. our
   3. their   6. My, His,
              or Our
C. Answers will vary.

Page 28

1. d   3. b   5. d   7. b   9. c
2. c   4. c   6. b   8. d   10. a

Page 29

A. 1. wrote   4. weave   7. tie   10. wished
   2. painted   5. knits   8. learned
   3. twisted   6. stretched   9. made
B. 1. hopped   2. pounded   3. slurped   4. sewed
C. Answers will vary.

Page 30

A. 1. use   3. imagine   5. amazes
   2. tie   4. invented
B. 1. lounge   3. gulp   5. staple
   2. gallop   4. drag

Page 31

A. 1. b   3. a   5. a
   2. c   4. b
B. 1. b   3. a   5. a
   2. b   4. b

Page 32

A. 1. past   5. present   9. future
   2. past   6. future   10. present
   3. future   7. present   11. past
   4. past   8. past
B. 1. Gum acted as an eraser.
   2. Unfortunately, pure rubber cracked in cold weather.
   3. Goodyear licensed the process to shoe companies.

Page 33

A. 1. wears   4. hurt   7. buys
   2. make   5. cause   8. want
   3. teaches   6. places
B. With Most Singular subjects: laces, designs, reaches, erases
   With Plural Subjects: lace, design, reach, erase

Page 34

A. 1. c   2. a   3. c   4. b   5. c
B. 1. a   2. c   3. b   4. a   5. c

Page 35

A. 1. will happen   6. will handle
   2. has equipped   7. was talking
   3. was polishing   8. had helped
   4. had tinkered   9. is wearing
   5. was gathering   10. will need
B. 1. had (asked); past   4. will (enjoy); future
   2. will (drop); future   5. has (eaten); past
   3. is (learning); present   6. are (taking); present

Page 36

A. 1. was cooking   4. is tasting
   2. had added   5. will add
   3. have prepared   6. have arrived
B. 1. will bake   4. had planted
   2. has picked   5. have tossed
   3. is picking   6. are planning
C. Answers will vary.

Page 37

1. a   3. c   5. b   7. b   9. a
2. a   4. a   6. c   8. b   10. c

Page 38

A. 1. (I) am (reader)
   2. (books) are (nonfiction)
   3. (bookstore) is (one)
   4. (books) are (interesting)
   5. (owner) is (knowledgeable)
   6. (name) is (Terry Baldes)
   7. (Mr. Baldes) was (inventor, scientist)
   8. (windows) were (attractive)
   9. (event) was (appearance)
   10. (friends) are (admirers)
B. 1. is   3. were   5. were
   2. was   4. are
C. Answers will vary.

Page 39

A. 1. was, S   5. were, P   9. were, P
   2. were, P   6. are, P   10. was, S
   3. are, P   7. is, S   11. am, S
   4. is, S   8. are, P
B. 1. is   2. are   3. are   4. is
C. Answers will vary.

Page 40

1. c   3. c   5. a   7. a   9. b
2. b   4. b   6. b   8. b   10. a

Page 41

A. 1. bought   4. rode   7. took
   2. made   5. shook   8. thought
   3. came   6. heard   9. broke
B. 1. heard   4. broke   7. shook
   2. made   5. rode
   3. bought   6. came

Page 42

A. 1. have chosen   6. have gone
   2. has brought   7. had heard
   3. have eaten   8. have ridden
   4. has hidden   9. has bought
   5. had taken
B. 1. heard   4. ridden   7. brought
   2. taken   5. chosen
   3. gone   6. bought

Page 43

A. 1. b   2. a   3. c   4. a   5. b
B. 1. a   2. c   3. a   4. b   5. c

Page 44

A. 1. (colorful), (dark); many
   2. (small); few
   3. (strange), (unusual); one
   4. (mysterious)
   5. (big), (dark); four
   6. (rare), (new)
   7. (tiny), (large), (cold)
   8. (amazing); several
B. Sample answers are given.
   1. small, mysterious
   2. big, large
   3. sandy, small, long
   4. new
   5. underwater, several, many
C. Answers will vary.

Page 45

A. Sample answers are given.
   1. big, hungry
   2. fuzzy, orange, little
   3. missing, tasty
   4. plastic, red; red-headed, young
   5. more, tasty, good
B. 1. gray, shaggy, dark   4. soft, shady
   2. some, droopy   5. enormous, large
   3. little, quiet
C. Answers will vary.

Page 46
1. a	3. b	5. a	7. a	9. b
2. c	4. b	6. b	8. a	10. c

Page 47
A.
1. older	4. quieter	7. brightest
2. loudest	5. higher	8. saddest
3. biggest	6. softer	

B.
1. hottest; more than two
2. warmer; two
3. colder; two
4. tallest; more than two
5. longer, two
6. friendliest; more than two
7. younger; two
8. liveliest; more than two

Page 48
1. funniest	7. more challenging
2. funnier	8. most challenging
3. busier	9. more tiring
4. busiest	10. most tiring
5. more exciting	11. more delicious
6. most exciting	12. most delicious

Page 49
1. a	3. b	5. a	7. a	9. a
2. b	4. a	6. b	8. a	10. b

Page 50
A.
1. of mountains, rivers, and lakes.
2. on the walls of his room
3. to the scenes in the pictures
4. on a camping trip
5. in a backpack and knapsack
6. from his father's mug
7. in the mountains for hours
8. at the Lost Lake
9. on their journey
10. at a quiet place for the night
11. in a tent
12. from the wind and rain
13. to his father
14. on their camping trip

B. Answers will vary.

Page 51
A.
1. in	3. on	5. at
2. with	4. for	6. into

B. Answers will vary.
C. Answers will vary.

Page 52
1. a	3. b	5. c	7. a	9. c
2. c	4. a	6. c	8. b	10. b

Page 53
A.
1. Tucker, lives; present
2. It, opens; present
3. Tucker, collected; past
4. mouse, filled; past
5. Tucker, sits; present
6. He, watches; present
7. boy, worked; past
8. They, sell; present

B.
1. crowd, passes; singular
2. Trains, run; plural
3. Papa, waits; singular
4. station, feels; singular
5. People, rush; plural
6. Mama, Papa, make; plural

Page 54
A.
1. Crickets, make
2. males, produce
3. I, listen
4. You, hear
5. Mario, finds
6. mother, calls

B.
1. Mario wants the cricket for a pet.
2. He wishes for a pet of his own.
3. Crickets seem like unusual pets to his mother.
4. Maybe insects scare her!

Page 55
A.
1. b	3. a	5. a
2. b	4. b	

B.
1. c	3. c	5. b
2. a	4. b	

Page 56
A.
1. "I really like tall tales!"
2. "Davy Crockett is my favorite character,"
3. "Who likes Sally Ann Thunder Ann Whirlwind?"

B.
1. "I am a big fan of hers."
2. I added, "Sally can even sing a wolf to sleep."
3. "How did Sally tame King Bear?"
4. "Sally really ought to be in the movies,"

C.
1. "What kind of person is Sally?" asked Davy Crockett.
2. The schoolmarm replied, "Sally is a special friend."
3. "She can laugh the bark off a pine tree," added Lucy.
4. The preacher said, "She can dance a rock to pieces."
5. "I'm very impressed!" exclaimed Davy.

D. Answers will vary.

Page 57
A.
1. "Well,	3. "Yes,
2. "Oh, Ed,	4. "Thank you,

B.
1. "Kim, your posters for the talent contest are terrific!"
2. She replied, "Thank you, Doug, for your kind words."
3. Our teacher asked, "Meg, will you play your guitar or sing?"
4. "Oh, I plan to do both," said Meg.
5. "Will you perform your juggling act this year Roberto?"
6. "No, I want to do a comedy routine,"

C.
1. "Kit, which act did you like best?" asked Mina.
2. He replied, "Oh, I enjoyed the singing pumpkins and the tap dancing elephants."
3. "Well, I liked the guitar player," said Mina.

D. Answers will vary.

Page 58
1. b	3. b	5. a	7. a	9. a
2. a	4. c	6. b	8. c	10. b

Page 59
A.
1. shouted, Later
2. hit, Yesterday
3. got, soon
4. tried, earlier
5. went, Then

B.
1. fell, everywhere
2. piled, up
3. were trapped, inside
4. tunneled, out
5. traveled, there

C.
1. never, when	3. inside, where
2. underground, where	4. Soon, when

Page 60
A.
1. talked, happily
2. squawked, sharply
3. greeted, warmly
4. guided, expertly
5. wrote, regularly
6. recorded, faithfully
7. responded, personally
8. looked, eagerly
9. jumped, quickly
10. snorkeled, easily
11. saw, clearly
12. gazed, intently
13. surrounded, Swiftly
14. chased and nipped, playfully

B. Sample answers are given.
1. bellowed loudly.   2. swam gracefully.

Page 61
A.
1. a	2. b	3. b	4. c	5. a

B.
1. c	2. b	3. a	4. a	5. b